TAKE SOMEONE WITH YOU

Gordon Moore

Ark House Press
PO Box 1722, Port Orchard, WA 98366 USA
PO Box 1321, Mona Vale NSW 1660 Australia
PO Box 318 334, West Harbour, Auckland 0661 New Zealand
arkhousepress.com

Cataloguing in Publication Data:
Title: Take Somebody With You
ISBN: 978-0-6486703-9-1 (pbk.)
Subjects: Leadership
Other Authors/Contributors: Moore, Gordon J

Published with Gordon J Moore
PO Box 46 Aspley Qld 4034 AUSTRALIA

CONTENTS

INTRODUCTION

One of the top questions asked of me by pastors and leaders has been: "If you had to choose, what three meetings in church life would you keep?"

This is a great question because the underlying thought behind it is: what should leaders focus their time, energy and resources on?

My answer is this. If I had to choose the top three, I'd go for Sunday services, the church prayer meeting and the leaders meeting, because from these three core activities, everything in church life flows!

Sunday services = celebration, worship and fellowship, attraction and conversion of the lost, preaching and teaching the Word of God to the whole congregation, casting of vision to members, supernatural ministry of the Holy Spirit to the church.

Prayer meeting = seeking God first, trust and reliance on Christ as Head of the church, God-consciousness made central to church life, unity of faith and purpose in church, supernatural and miraculous engagement by members.

Leaders meeting = establishment of spiritual authority, 'chain of command' and accountability beyond the senior leader, the appointment and mobilisation of the leadership team to influence the church and beyond, the endorsing, empowering and training of leaders for effectiveness, the fulfillment of the calling, purpose, values and culture of the church through a unified leadership team.

Leadership development must be one of the top priorities of senior leadership in any church or organisation because every organisation rises and falls according to the level of leadership.

Deep in the heart of the concept of *Take Someone With You* is the value of raising leaders from within the church. This mindset of leadership understands that the health and the growth of the church is in the **let them** concept:

> *"Enlarge the place of your tent,*
> *and **let them** stretch forth the curtains of*
> *your habitations:*
> *spare not, lengthen your cords, and strengthen*
> *your stakes;*
> *For you shall break forth on the right hand and*
> *on the left;*
> *and your seed shall inherit the Gentiles,*
> *and make the desolate cities to be inhabited."*

Isaiah 54:2-4

Every leader has a limit to what they can physically do, so the raising of leaders multiplies that reality and effectiveness.

At its core, the concept of *Take Someone With You* works like this...

WIN LOST PEOPLE
MAKE DISCIPLES
RAISE LEADERS

...who...

WIN LOST PEOPLE
MAKE DISCIPLES
RAISE LEADERS

...who...

WIN LOST PEOPLE
MAKE DISCIPLES
RAISE LEADERS

...who...

I trust this book will inspire you to commit your leadership priorities to raising leaders around you as you *Take Someone With You*.

Gordon Moore
AUTHOR

CHAPTER ONE:

CREATING A LEADERSHIP CULTURE

Culture is a way of thinking, behaving, or working that exists in a group, place or organisation. Culture is the sum of attitudes, customs, and beliefs that distinguishes one group of people from another.

Culture = what we value
Culture = what we practise
Culture = what attitudes we hold
Culture = what we actually do

'Shared culture' is what we do, or our behaviour, when we're not together. This is because culture is more than what we would like to do; it is a deeply shared belief that has changed our behaviour. Culture is what people experience.

Culture does not equal what we WANT
Culture does not equal what we BELIEVE
Culture does not equal what we REQUIRE
Culture does not equal what we TEACH

Culture is the atmosphere in which vision and purpose is developed and flourishes because without the right culture, vision and purpose are hindered and disabled.

How then is culture developed?

Leadership Sets Culture

Culture is learned. It is not biological; we do not inherit it and much of learning culture is subconscious or organic.

We learn culture from families, peers, institutions, media and of course, leaders.

The process of learning culture is known as 'enculturation', which is derived from the agricultural concept of cultivation.

Therefore, we observe that culture takes time to grow. Once the 'tree of culture' is established, its fruit is perpetual.

Culture is shaped by how leaders act and behave, so it is essential that leaders and their leadership teams embody, demonstrate, live and promote the type of culture they want to see.

All leaders must understand that culture is shaped by a consistency of message and practice because culture is dynamic as it interacts with other cultures. This is why leadership must constantly reinforce, repeat and endorse the desired culture.

So, is a 'teamwork culture' the ideal? Then you will need to make sure your executive team truly works as a team.

Is 'transparency' important? Guess what, your leaders will need to be transparent - even when it's difficult.

Is the benefit and success in life of members the goal? Then every leader on team must be working to enhance and boost the benefit and success of the church members. There can be no accommodating and including of leaders who are not engendering, endorsing and promoting the desired culture.

Leaders and key influencers need to fit with the core values

A 'Culture of Requirement' versus a 'Shared Culture'

Creating a 'culture of requirement' as opposed to a 'shared culture' can be observed in a church, for example, when members are required to serve on a welcoming roster and to be friendly and smile. However, when people leave the roster and go home, they are no longer friendly!

An example of this is a popular sushi restaurant chain in Australia, where employees are obviously trained and required to give a 'friendly greeting' to every customer who enters their restaurant. However, because they did not 'make friends' with their customers, the friendliness of the employees stops when their shift concludes. This is the creation of a 'friendly culture' by requirement as opposed to a 'friendship-making culture' that extends beyond the employment environment.

This can be true in a church environment where a 'friendship-making culture' is far better, in terms of health and growth, than a required 'friendly culture'. Our friendliness must extend beyond our roster service, or ministry, or function and become a shared culture that we are living out, wherever we are.

The problem with a 'Requiring Culture', that is an enforced conformity, is the creation of the very opposite to what we desire, want or teach.

For example, if evangelism is adopted as a 'requirement' then members will only perform in the program to meet expectations but as soon as they go home, or go to work, they connect with no one! This is because they can feel that they have 'done their evangelism', rather than living evangelistically as a shared culture.

How to create Culture

Culture is created by leaders who, first of all, engender the desired culture by what they do. This is the way that leaders set the culture by providing clear, observable and practical examples of the desired culture.

Without speaking a word, they are addressing and removing practices and attitudes that create a contrary culture. People learn and know the culture by imitating and following their leader's example.

> *"Be imitators of me, just as I also am of Christ."*
> *1 Corinthians 11:1 (NET)*

Once this is being done, it is vital that leaders strengthen their actions and example by teaching culture in such a way that inspires adoption of the desired culture and makes heroes out of those who also engender the culture. Communication is greatly enhanced when leaders emphasise the 'why' of culture; the reasons why we do what we do.

CHAPTER TWO:

PROGRESSING DISCIPLES

To be successful at raising leaders, there must first be an underlying value and practice of progressing people.

In the Book of Acts, the first six chapters reveal a progressive terminology for members of the early church. Luke, the writer, develops a changing view and terminology of the members as they progressed in their spiritual journey.

The first three words define the phase of establishment and the connecting and building of the new members into the community of faith:

- **Acts 2:41 – "Souls"**, Luke refers to these first members, who responded to the invitation of Peter, as "Souls". He states that they were "added" and we can see three things about these "Souls":

  - They were people or individuals

  - They were initiated into the church through their personal encounter with God

  - They were connected to the church and the Christian life through members of the church ("added to them")

- **Acts 4:32 – "Believers"**, who we now see taking further steps of commitment into the community of the church. Luke defines these believers as possessing "One Heart and Soul", and so we can see three things about these "believers":

  - they have been established into "the faith" ("believers")

- they have committed to a kingdom lifestyle

- they are actively part of the church community

- **Acts 6:1 – "Disciples"**, we now see a stronger definition used as the believers progress into becoming "disciples". We observe three key things about disciples:

  - Disciples multiply the church

  - Disciples are learners and students

  - Disciples are defined as "discipled ones", that is, in a process of growth and change

Acts chapter six is a pivotal chapter in the early church because it is the first occasion where the church intentionally got organised to cope with the growth, as well as the conflicts that arose due to the growth.

In this chapter, Luke introduces the new concept of "**servants**", or "**deacons**", from the Greek word *"diakoneo" (Strong's Concordance G1247)*, which is variously translated "attendant, to act as a deacon, to minister".

In modern English, we would understand this term referred to a new office of 'assistant leaders' to the apostles. The Amplified Bible is helpful when it uses the words, *"serving tables and **superintending** the distribution of foods"* and *"we may assign to look after this business and duty"*.

This language indicates that this was an 'oversight role' not just a 'doing role'. We can observe the emergence of a new level of responsibility and function in the early church, which revealed the kind of appointments that the apostles must have made in other areas as well to cope with the growth and expansion of the church.

It is evident in the following two chapters of Acts, which highlight Stephen the Prophet (Acts 7) and Phillip the Evangelist (Acts 8), that these 'ministers' were not just practical in their ministry but were also accomplished preachers and ministers of the Word of God.

The word 'deacon' is also used to recognize Phoebe's ministry as the first female deacon to the church in Cenchrea (Romans 16:1).

Later in his writings, the Apostle Paul summarises the significance and quality of 'deacon leadership' by outlining the qualifications of deacons in 1 Timothy 3:8-13.

As we trace this development of the progression of members in the early church, we observe another significant introduction of the terms "**Prophets & Teachers**" in Acts 13:1, which is given to define the **leaders** of the church in Antioch.

What is interesting to note is that these leaders are not part of the original group of apostles in Jerusalem, however, they held the same level of authority and function of leadership in the church in Antioch as the 12 apostles did in the church in Jerusalem.

These men were leading the local church together at Antioch in their own right and authority from which the apostles Barnabas and Saul were launched out into other cities and countries in church leadership and ministry.

The Five New Testament Levels of Leadership Development

- **Souls**
- **Believers**
- **Disciples**
- **Ministers**
- **Leaders**

We can also view these 5 levels, or stages of progress, in members from a kingdom perspective in the following way:

- **Souls** – are '**IN** the Kingdom'
- **Believers** – '**SEE** the Kingdom'
- **Disciples** – are '**OF** the Kingdom'
- **Ministers** – are '**FOR** the Kingdom'
- **Leaders** – '**ARE** the Kingdom'

This journey of discipleship, from a 'soul' to a 'leader', moves me and progresses me from being "me in the Kingdom", to being "the Kingdom in and through me".

This is an important distinction to make because it identifies our goal as leaders, which is to create an environment in which people can progress in their journey of faith.

Motivations of each Phase:

With each phase, or level of growth, as we progress in our journey of faith, we can identify the following changes in our motivations:

'Souls' – "Me"

We all come to Christ so aware of our needs, lacks and desperate situations. Our common theme song could be titled, "Jesus help me!"

'Believers' – "My faith"

Once we are established as new believers, we figure out that our faith can actually work for us and we begin to focus on how we can develop our faith even more.

'Disciples' – "His servant"

Becoming a disciple of Christ is our next step as we find ourselves moving from 'me' and 'my', to 'Him'!

We now embrace servanthood. This dramatic change in us shifts us from Jesus meeting our needs, to us meeting Jesus' needs. We have become His servant!

'Ministers' – "Adding value to His agenda"

Discipleship propels us to yet another level when we realise that we are trained and equipped 'ministers' who can actually add value to others as we find opportunity to make a difference in people's lives.

'Leaders' – "Influence others to progress and add value"

This is the highest level of motivation as a Christian. When we embrace leadership, we are no longer motivated and rewarded by what we do, but rather by empowering and equipping others to discover their purpose and contribution to Christ by adding value to others. This is the level of multiplication.

How to progress and transition disciples

What are the catalysts that progress members from one level to the next?

'Souls to Believers' – Experiencing a supernatural and life-transforming encounter with God (the New Birth) will propel the 'Soul' into a 'Believer' because of the establishment of personal faith in God.

'Believers to Disciples' – This is an important transition to make and probably one of the most significant because progress will not occur if we don't make this transition. This is where the newly-established believer discovers the need to change. Up until this stage, God has accepted us as we are. He saves us, gives us gifts and sets our path ahead of us. However, we soon discover that not all our habits, attitudes, motivations and actions are kingdom-promoting. God, therefore, will not leave us where He found us. He will lead us to 'points of discipleship' that challenge and confront us with the reality that we need to change! This is where we must become a 'disciple' – a pupil, a learner and a disciplined person. In other words, what began as miraculous and automatic (the New Birth), now must become practical and manual with our cooperation through the practice of obedience and self discipline... 'discipleship'.

'Disciples to Ministers' – there are two essential attributes that we can identify that shifts disciples into becoming ministers. The first is 'servanthood'. Servanthood is vital because we cannot be effective in Christ's kingdom until we have personally embraced **humility**, which means we have submitted to someone else and their agenda. Someone once said, "No one minds being a servant until someone treats you like one!" To allow someone else to decide, direct, require, instruct and command means I have a humble spirit. I respect leadership and willingly submit and flow to fulfil purposes and outcomes that are greater than myself. This is true Christian ministry at its core.

The second important attribute that shifts us into ministry is the **discovery of gifts**, talents and skills that add value to people and the Kingdom. The role of leadership is not to simply hold a position or exercise authority, but rather to use that position and authority to empower people in such a way that they discover their gifts and skills and are mobilised into effective ministry.

'**Ministers to Leaders**' – This is the highest level of Christianity, in my view, because a minister becomes a leader when they have become truly selfless and others-centered. This transition happens when a 'minister' develops the ability to not just exercise their own ministry, but rather to empower, progress and facilitate others into their ministries. With this comes the ability to take responsibility and exercise spiritual authority. It is easy to see how dangerous it can be for individuals to assume spiritual leadership without first of all embracing servanthood. This is the meaning behind the words of Jesus:

> *"And if you have not been faithful in that which is another man's,*
> *who shall give you that which is your own?"*
> *Luke 16:12*

The test of authentic spiritual leadership is not just about how influential, educated, connected or gifted we are, but rather how faithfully and humbly we have served under the leaders God has appointed over us!

Ministry is such an important phase of development for every Christian, because it prepares and qualifies us for leadership. Therefore, we should never be in a hurry to by pass or short cut the process. Ministry will develop humility and faithfulness in us like nothing else!

The proving ground for leadership is found in the faithfulness of serving another leader

Observe the instruction of the apostle Paul regarding the selection and appointment of ministers, or deacons:

> "**Not a novice**, lest being lifted up with pride
> he fall into the condemnation of the devil...
> ...And let these also **first be proved**;
> then let them use the office of a **deacon**,
> being found blameless."
> *1 Timothy 3:6,10*

The progression of disciples can be summarised in the following chart:

REFERENCE	ACTS 2:4	ACTS 4:32	ACTS 6:1	ACTS 6:2-3	ACTS 13:1
DESCRIPTION	"SOULS"	"BELIEVERS"	"DISCIPLES"	"MINISTERS"	"LEADERS"
DYNAMIC	"ADDED"	"UNIFIED"	"MULTIPLY"	"SERVING"	"DIRECTING"
TRANSITION PRINCIPLE	PERSONAL FAITH	POINTS OF DISCIPLESHIP	SERVANTHOOD & GIFTS	RESPONSIBILITY & FACILITATE OTHERS	
MIRACLE	'MIRACLE OF ENTRANCE'	'MIRACLE OF ESTABLISHING'	MIRACLE OF REMAINING	MIRACLE OF HUMILITY	MIRACLE OF AUTHORITY
SPIRITUAL DOORS	REPENTANCE	COMMITTMENT	SUBMISSION	HUMILITY	OBEDIENCE
KINGDOM FOCUS	IN KINGDOM	SEE KINGDOM	OF KINGDOM	FOR KINGDOM	ARE KINGDOM
LEADERSHIP FOCUS	WINNING	PASTORING	TEACHING	COACHING	MENTORING
LANGUAGE	"ME"	"MY FAITH"	"HIS SERVANT"	"ADD VALUE"	"INFLUENCE"
LEADERSHIP APPROACH	INCLUDING	GROUNDING	TEACHING	TRAINING	DEVELOPING

The Four Quadrants of Progressing People

When we view the progression of disciples from an operational perspective, we can observe that people progress through the following four levels of serving and leading:

QUADRANTS

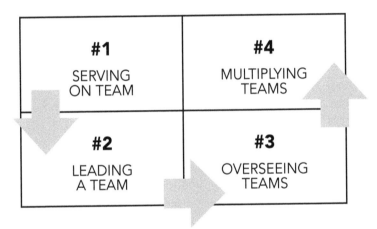

This quadrant grid is helpful because it shows how people develop and progress in their leadership ability.

The first thing to notice is that most leaders don't start out as leaders. Leaders start out as a member of a team, serving in some capacity (quadrant 1), learning skills and developing leadership capacity. The secret for effective leadership development is to create as many opportunities as possible for people to serve in quadrant 1. This is achieved by breaking down serving roles into as many 'doable tasks' as possible and so creating the opportunities for people to serve on team.

As people serve on team, leaders are better positioned to be able to observe and to identify those that are showing potential leadership traits and to then move them to leading a team (quadrant 2), where the level of training on the job, coaching and mentoring is intensified.

As leaders become effective by growing and multiplying their team, they can be moved to the next level on the grid of overseeing teams (quadrant 3). The best overseers of teams are those that have effectively led and grown teams because they have an 'on the job', practical knowledge of leading healthy teams.

The next level of leadership is discovered when a leader begins to develop and multiply overseers under them, creating a dynamic of multiplication through the whole organisation through 'overseeing overseers'. This is the highest level of leadership as this kind of leader knows how to recruit, mobilise and train volunteers to serve on teams (quadrant 1), mentor and develop leaders (quadrant 2), and empower overseers (quadrant 3).

Some Key Questions to assist moving people through the quadrants:

- Where am I currently positioned on the quadrant?
- Where do I need to develop and grow to move to the next quadrant?
- Where are others positioned and functioning on the grid around me?

- Where do they need to develop and grow to move to the next quadrant?

Building an effective 'Leadership Track'

The leadership development system can be defined as the 'Leadership Track'. To design, implement and articulate a leadership track for your church is just as important as developing a new member track, because it is the continuation of the new member's progress in their faith journey.

The components of such a leadership development system, which includes the linking of all the evangelism and disciple-making processes in the church, involves the following:

- Winning lost people
- Establishing new members in the faith
- Identifying every member's gifts and passions
- Mobilising members into serving on teams
- Providing on-the-job training, coaching and mentoring
- Mobilising leaders to lead teams
- Appointing overseers to coordinate and facilitate

CHAPTER THREE:

RAISING LEADERS FROM WITHIN

A mistake we can all make is to view leadership development as a separate process to disciple-making and overlook the vital connection that exists between raising leaders and progressing members through the life of the church.

Creating a Culture of 'Next Steps'

The ultimate goal for every believer is to progress to become a leader – an influencer, encourager, empowerer and a developer of others – whether officially appointed or not.

> *"For although by this time you should be teachers, you again need to have someone teach you the rudiments of the first principles of the oracles of God."*
>
> *Hebrews 5:12 (WEB)*

This is the creation of a 'disciples making disciples' culture. In other words, every member is part of the 'next steps' culture, which is seeking to influence, encourage, endorse, promote, equip and help every member within their sphere of influence to take their next step towards leadership. This is leadership culture at work!

The ability to raise leaders is in direct proportion to the ability to mobilise members into service, which is in direct proportion to the ability to make disciples, which is in direct proportion to the ability to win lost people.

This process is summarised as follows:

- Conversion and assimilation of unsaved people
- Disciple-making
- Mobilisation into service
- Raising Leaders

If the '80/20 principle' is correct, it would be reasonable to expect that for every 100 decisions for Christ at the 'front door' of the church, there would be at least 20 trained and mobilised leaders functioning at the end of the process (given that leadership training and mentoring is effective).

Raising leaders from within the church is the key to effectiveness and fruitfulness

The Three Methods of Raising Leaders

The first method of raising leaders is the process of recruiting leaders from 'outside'. This is a common practice found in many churches, where no leadership pathway actually exists, and so, leaders are recruited from outside the church. The focus of recruiting from 'outside' is the appointing of leaders who already possess talents and skills beyond any leader within the church.

The PROS of recruiting from outside

Recruiting from outside gives the senior leader a quick fix for lacks and gaps in the church organisation and in the existing team. This then means there is no need to put in time and effort into the identifying, coaching, mentoring and training of potential leaders from within the church.

The CONS of recruiting from outside

The main effect of recruiting from outside is that existing team members can often feel overlooked and disempowered and as a result, may pull back or leave to go where they will feel valued.

The biggest problem with this approach is that leaders brought in from the outside without a process of intentional assimilation, bring with them their own purpose, culture, values and style (and issues) that have been developed elsewhere. This would be one of the most overlooked aspects of leadership recruitment. As a result, this new and often contrary culture can gradually grow, influence and cause potential conflict within the leadership team and church community.

The second method of raising leaders is the process of raising leaders from 'beside'. This approach, the 'safe approach', recruits and appoints leaders from among friends and peers from across and within the organisation.

The PROS of recruiting from beside

The reason this is termed the 'safe' method is because such appointments are made from among proven and safe known friends, peers and colleagues from across the organisation.

The obvious benefit of such a strategy is that there is no need to train the incumbents extensively because they already know what to do as they are well acquainted with the operations of the organisation.

The result of such appointments is that the risk factor is greatly reduced.

The CONS of recruiting from beside

The major problem with only recruiting from 'beside' is that a 'closed leadership group' is formed which can lead to the diminishing of innovation and new ideas within the organisation. Over time, adoption of safe and narrow viewpoints can emerge which can stifle growth and progress.

However, the mid to long-term issue is that the senior team of the church gradually grows old together making succession a more difficult prospect because the recruitment pool of 'Next-Gens' becomes smaller and smaller.

This can create an environment where young leaders keep leaving because no leadership pathway is visible or possible.

Finally, authority issues can emerge because peers and friends can feel an equality and familiarity with the senior leader.

The third method of raising leaders is the process of raising leaders from 'beneath'.

This approach centers on the identifying, recruiting, coaching, mentoring and training of potential leaders from 'beneath' the leader and within the organisation.

The PROS of recruiting from beneath

First of all, loyalty and commitment to the senior leader, team and the church are high and unquestioned because leaders recruited from within have already proven themselves over time. The existing purpose, values and culture of the church remain strong and consistent, resulting in unity and harmony in the leadership team and church.

Secondly, there is a high level of buy-in and willingness to learn because leaders raised from within the church have been discipled over a long period of time and generally possess a servant attitude towards leadership and the church family.

Thirdly, authority challenges and conflicts are greatly reduced because of an established culture and understanding of respect and honour from both senior leadership and the new leaders.

Fourthly, high levels of fresh energy, ideas and innovation are brought to the leadership team because of the injection of young, fresh perspectives, views and voices.

Fifthly, longevity and stability occurs in the team and church because 'sons and daughters' tend to stay with their father and mother. Roles and positions are viewed through the lens of 'home' and 'family' rather than a 'job', or a 'position'.

Sixthly, future succession is made much smoother because of the large pool of quality young leaders that are present within the church with high degrees of loyalty to each other and the team.

The CONS of recruiting from beneath

Firstly, recruiting from beneath is slower and doesn't offer a 'quick fix' to lacks and needs within the organisation.

Secondly, this approach takes a lot of time, energy and effort to raise leaders from beneath.

Thirdly, there is a higher risk factor because new, younger leaders will make mistakes in their journey to maturity and competence.

Fourthly, existing, older and often more experienced leaders may feel insecure and threatened by younger leaders rising above them. Especially when the new, younger leader has previously served in a position beneath them in the organisation and has now been promoted to lead in a position above them.

This is a very important issue that must be addressed if senior leaders and churches are serious about raising leaders from within the church.

This can be addressed by creating a culture where the established and older leaders exist to ensure the empowerment and success of younger leaders, and where the younger leaders respect and honour the older leaders.

The Key Attitudes for Raising Leaders

The adoption of four key attitudes is crucial in the raising of leaders from within the church.

Firstly, every member and leader in the church must hold the core conviction that the church's future health; development and growth are vested in the raising of next generation leaders.

The sayings, "If we don't raise the next generation we'll be dead in the next generation" and "The older I become, the more responsible I become to raise the next generation", hold true.

Secondly, humility of heart creates an environment and attitude that empowers and releases others, especially the younger generations. Sometimes older leaders need to recognise that they have had a fair go at leadership, won't be there forever and therefore need to make room for new younger leaders. Otherwise, how else will young leaders flourish and develop if opportunity is not given to them?

Thirdly, the adoption of a 'parental' view by older leaders and members is critical because what parent doesn't want to see their children flourish and be successful; even supersede them?

Fourthly, younger leaders can play an important role by exercising humility and the honouring of the older, more experienced and wiser leaders.

The concept of raising leaders is not about creating a young, one-generation leadership environment, but rather, a family of all generations working together to build God's House!

"Rebuke not an elder, but entreat him as a father;
and the younger men as brothers;
the elder women as mothers;
the younger as sisters, with all purity."
1 Timothy 5:1-2

CHAPTER FOUR:

LEADING FROM THE FRONT ROW

"It's not who's sitting in the back row; it's who's sitting in the front row that makes a church great."

It took me a long time to work out that when I got the church 'front row' right, I would get the church right.

What I found myself focusing on continually as a senior leader was, "who's turning up", "who's not turning up", "who's leaving" and "who's joining".

Somehow I got caught up in the misconception that my success as a leader was being leeched away by every departure. Then it dawned on me: people will always leave! It's the nature of people and church; it's the way it is.

Here's the thing: You can't stop people from leaving, but you can help the great people that are with you **stay**.

Once I began to concentrate on investing into the lives of the awesome people that I did have with me, we literally saw our church progress and grow before our eyes.

What I was doing was putting all my focus, concerns and energy into the 'back row' of the church, rather than focusing on who was there and finding ways to make things happen with these great people that God had already given me: the 'front row'.

As a result of this realisation, I have come to understand the power of these two key principles about raising leaders:

- Build with who you have, not with who you don't have.

- The stronger the front row, the stronger the church.

As a result of this journey as a leader, I arrived at a place of understanding that I'm not responsible for who and what I don't have; neither should I worry about it!

Therefore, our job as leaders is to accept the responsibility of raising leaders from within our church and work with who and what God has already given us instead of looking over the fence and comparing ourselves to others based on what they have.

> *"If I am not an apostle to others, **at least I am to you**, for you are the confirming sign of my apostleship in the Lord."*
> *1 Corinthians 9:2*

The secret to raising leaders is to work on identifying, empowering and developing the 'front row' of your church, and then watch your church flourish.

Your ultimate success as a leader is determined by who stays with you

The 'A Team' is your Front Row

As you embark on this exciting journey of empowering and raising leaders, you will observe the emergence of your 'A Team' – the key leaders who commit over the long term and will work with you in building the church.

These 'A Team' players will fulfill many roles and functions over time as the church grows and develops, and so, change is inevitable. I describe this as being like riding on a bus. There are many of us on the bus, and some may change seats over time, but we're still riding on the same bus towards the same destination.

The Five Most Important Questions we must Answer as Leaders

- What is our **compelling purpose** for our leadership team?

- Have we got the right **people** on the team?

- Have we given the team the right **structure** so it can work?

- Do we give the team the right **support** it needs to succeed?

- Are we **coaching the team** in order to improve team effectiveness?

Before you can effectively lead a team, you need to be clear about **what you're doing**…and **not doing**. This is why it is vital that your role must be interpreted and implemented according to the size, level and stage of your church (see my books "Leadership Styles & Levels of Church" and "Going to the Next Level").

Practical Steps to begin Raising Leaders

Define your role

Begin with yourself as senior leader and list the 4 main roles or functions you must fulfill in order to be effective as the senior leader of your church.

Define the roles and activities that build the church

What are the critical areas, the 'must haves', in order to grow the church?

Key questions:

- What type of people do you want to reach? Who are the people in your community? (suggested reading: "Raving Fans", by Ken Blanchard)

- What are the needs in your community?

- Where is your current growth coming from? In other words, what departments/programs are actually growing the church? (Sunday services; special events such as Easter, Christmas, Father's/Mother's Day; Youth events, Children's events, Young Families events etc.)

- Who is creating your current growth – promote and move these 'growth agents' into key roles in your team

Match the roles to the right people

The next important step is to understand the people you have and to match each person to the role that they are best suited for in order to maximise the health and growth of the church.

Sometimes there will be the need to shift people from their role while others will be brought in to assume a role that they are better suited to.

Evidence of fruitfulness, success, and the necessary skill set that match a particular role is vital

Provide a structure that facilitates the effective working of the team

Once the team is placed in the right functions, time needs to be given to develop a structure in which the team can effectively work together to produce maximum results.

The key components to give attention to in creating this kind of structure are:

- Team culture and protocols
- Meetings for feedback and strategic planning
- Coaching and training schedule for improvement in team performance
- Calendar of events and activities

Communicate, Communicate, Communicate

Communication must occur at all levels for the successful raising up of leaders.

The key leaders need to receive direct communication from you, the senior leader, both verbal and written, in order to fully understand the nature of their role, so they will be able to effectively communicate to their sphere of influence.

Follow up

(See Chapter Eleven)

CHAPTER FIVE:

LEADER, GET OUT OF THE WAY!

One of the most important keys to raising leaders is to provide multiple opportunities within the organisation for potential leaders to develop. This must happen from the car park to the pulpit. Which is to say, at every level, department, ministry and part of the church, there must be opportunities created for potential leaders to experience leading at the next level.

However, one of the biggest blockages to raising leaders is the leader! This is because the leader is found in the centre of everything, doing everything, present at everything, deciding everything, approving everything and as a result, there is no room for anyone else!

When this style of leadership occurs as a culture throughout the whole church, from the head deacon to the senior leader, there will be no raising up of new leaders. Key number one: leader, get out of the way!

There can be many reasons why leaders don't, won't, or can't, get out of the way and empower others. First of all, leaders may feel that they are really good at what they do and are convinced that no one else can produce the results and outcomes that he/she can, and so, they keep doing it themselves.

However, simple math comes into play here. Imagine, instead of one highly talented and gifted leader performing a role at 70-80% (because no one's perfect), what if five other leaders could be identified, trained, coached and empowered to perform the same role at 50%? Even though it may not be performed as well as the leader, that would produce 250% of what one leader can do by themselves! This is where training, coaching and mentoring kicks in to develop these 5 leaders to say 70%... now that's 350%!

We have discovered that it is essential to create an environment where it is ok to fail and not be perfect. This is the difference between perfectionism and excellence.

Perfectionism is the demand for everything to be perfect, by setting high and unrealistic standards at every moment of time, whereas, excellence is the constant pursuit of increasing improvements, step by step, over time.

Perfectionism crushes people's efforts because they can never measure up to the unrealistic standards and expectations put before them, whereas excellence encourages people to have another attempt, to learn, to adjust, to grow and progress from 50% to 60% and from 70% to 80%.

Secondly, most leaders really like what they do and find significance in what they do and just can't give it to others. I often hear leaders say, "This is my calling, this is what I'm supposed to do, and I love doing it!"

However, we all need to ask ourselves this question as leaders: Is my purpose as a leader to do MY ministry, or, is my purpose as a leader to empower others to do THEIR ministry?

If I'm so busy as a leader focusing on doing my ministry, then, I'm not leading others; I'm ministering to others!

MINISTRY = ME DOING
LEADERSHIP = EMPOWERING OTHERS TO DO

Thirdly, many leaders believe that if they do themselves out of their job, they'll have nothing to do. But this is far from the truth! When we commit ourselves as leaders to be constantly giving away responsibility and ministry opportunities to others, we will find ourselves busy enough providing the necessary training, coaching and mentoring in developing others.

Fourthly, many leaders don't know how to coach, mentor and raise up others. But anyone can learn how to become better at empowering and raising up others, even, if not perfectly.

CHAPTER SIX:

THE OPERATIONAL AND MENTORING STRATEGY

The key to effective leadership development is the creation of two complementary structures that run side by side in church life. These two structures can be defined as the 'operational structure' and the 'mentoring structure'.

The Railway Tracks of Operational and Mentoring Strategy

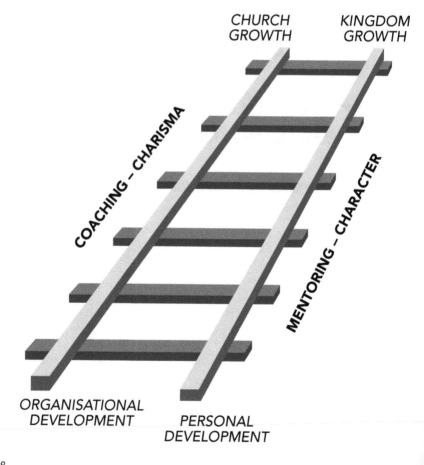

CHURCH GROWTH

KINGDOM GROWTH

COACHING – CHARISMA

MENTORING – CHARACTER

ORGANISATIONAL DEVELOPMENT

PERSONAL DEVELOPMENT

The operational structure focuses on the building of the church, while the mentoring structure focuses on the building of the leader.

The operational structure seeks to develop the leadership effectiveness of the leader, while the mentoring structure seeks to develop the discipleship effectiveness of the leader.

The operational structure prioritises the implementation of the vision of the church, while the mentoring structure prioritises the vision of the kingdom.

The operational structure develops the gifts, skills and abilities of the leader in the context of the church ministry and organisation, while the mentoring structure develops the spirituality, attitudes, motivations and traits of the leader in the context of the kingdom of God.

The implementation of an effective operational structure will develop the gifts, skills and talents of leaders but this is not enough to raise 'kingdom leaders'.

The operational structure involves activities such as vision, goals and outcomes, strategic planning, organisation, management, job descriptions, team building, coaching, training, feedback and evaluation.

The mentoring structure has a different focus and involves activities such as in-depth, personalised teaching and explanation, prayer, discussion, Q&A, impartation, guidance and correction.

Summary of the Necessary Shifts to Empower People

In order to become effective in developing people through a mentoring approach, the following shifts are needed:

- Moving from curriculum to relationship

- Moving from didactic teaching to intern training

- Moving from teaching about the job to training on the job

- Moving from being principle-based to practice-based

- Moving from ideas (theory) to implementation (practice)

- Moving from the head to the heart of the leader

Implementing a Mentoring Strategy

Every leader in the executive and HOD levels (heads of departments/ministries) of the church are included by invitation in this mentoring structure, or 'D-Group' (Discipleship Group) activity.

As part of our church mentoring structure, we regularly ran these 'D-Groups' on a 6-8 week basis throughout the year from February to November. In between the weeks when D-Groups are held, informal 'one-on-one' meetings are held with every individual usually over a coffee or around a meal.

We also found it beneficial to run separate male and female groups as well as two or three combined meetings throughout the year to build team through social activities and to cover general mentoring topics that benefit all the leaders.

These combined meetings often involve downloads from the senior leader, or an invited guest, who has proven expertise in a particular area.

Overview of some of the Key Topics/Areas Covered in D-Groups

- Devotional life: prayer, Scripture reading and meditation
- Character, morals and ethics development
- Dreams, goals, gifts, calling, personality and ministry
- Career and future
- Finances and wealth creation
- Relationships, marriage and family
- Lifestyle, health and fitness
- Doctrine and theology
- Church vision, purpose, core values and culture

The one-on-one meetings revolve around discussion, Q&A and follow-up on the topic covered in the D-Group from the individual leader's context, needs and questions.

CHAPTER SEVEN:

LEADERS ARE GOLD PROSPECTORS

What is our compelling purpose as leaders? What motivates us to keep turning up to do what we do? The answer to these questions is explained in the 'Great Commission' of Christ and in the instruction of the apostle Paul:

> *"All power is given unto me in heaven and in earth.*
> *Go therefore, and teach all nations, baptising them in*
> *the name of the Father,*
> *and of the Son, and of the Holy Spirit:*
> *Teaching them to observe all things whatsoever I*
> *have commanded you."*
> *Matthew 28:18-20*

> *"And the things that you have heard of me among*
> *many witnesses,*
> *the same commit to faithful men, who shall be able to*
> *teach others also."*
> *2 Timothy 2:2*

Our compelling reason, besides obeying the commands of Christ, is the incredible people that God brings to us with whom we get the privilege of doing life together. We have found gold!

In essence, our compelling reason can be put this way:

WIN LOST PEOPLE
MAKE DISCIPLES
GROW LEADERS...

who

WIN LOST PEOPLE
MAKE DISCIPLES
GROW LEADERS...

who

WIN LOST PEOPLE
MAKE DISCIPLES
GROW LEADERS

In order to win lost people, make disciples, and raise leaders, we have to be like gold prospectors, because most people don't look like leaders when they start out on their Christian journey.

I know I didn't! But leaders saw things in me that I didn't see, encouraged and developed me and gave me opportunities to serve, grow and progress. That's why I do what I do...I'm just passing on the favour!

The first thing every leader must do is dig for the gold in people.

Prospectors basically use three methods to find gold. Firstly, they use history, science and geology to work out where the gold is most likely to be. Secondly, they pan and use electronic detectors on the surface in those likely areas and, thirdly, they dig below the surface using diggers, or go even deeper, cutting shafts deep inside the earth to find the gold. Sometimes we have to dig a little deeper to find the gold in people.

The second thing to do in order to uncover the gold in people, is that every leader must be fully convinced and persuaded that **every** believer has 'gold' in them, or in other words, gifts and talents given to them by the Holy Spirit.

*"For by the grace given to me I say to
every one of you
not to think more highly of yourself than
you ought to think,
but to think with sober discernment,
as God has distributed to each of you a
measure of faith."
Romans 12:3 NET*

*To each person the manifestation of the Spirit is
given for the benefit of all."
1 Corinthians 12:7 NET*

The third thing about prospecting for gold in people is that you have to deal with a lot of dirt in order to find the gold.

Most new believers, who are not natural leaders and do not promote their own abilities because they are unaware of such giftings and anointings, need the insight, help and guidance of leaders to unearth their gifts.

This is the incredible privilege given to every leader: to help new believers find their gifts and callings, and to provide opportunities for the expression and contribution of their gifts in the life of the church family that they are now part of.

CHAPTER EIGHT:

THE ICEBERG OF LEADERSHIP

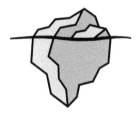

What sank the Titanic ocean liner? The iceberg they saw? Or, the iceberg they didn't see?

Of course, the answer is, "the iceberg they didn't see." This is also true for leadership.

One of the reasons why leaders can fail to be effective is not because of what the leader does visibly through their public ministry activity, but rather, his/her failure to do all those things that need to be done invisibly, or not in public leadership activity.

The true test of leadership is not about what happens when the leader is present, but rather, what happens when the leader isn't present.

Here's the reality that all leaders must face: sooner or later you will be absent from church, department or ministry because of holidays, commitments, sickness, or retirement. So you might as well purposefully plan and position yourself for such absences by identifying, training and releasing others to do the job, and especially, when you're not there.

Focusing on the unseen components of leadership, rather than focusing on the seen components of ministry will help you achieve this.

Ministry is obvious to everyone because by its very nature it is highly visible; for example, preaching, teaching, prophesying, song leading, chairing a meeting, counseling, praying for the sick, or leading a small group. Whereas leadership is not always obvious to everyone, because it involves behind the scenes activities such as interviewing, coaching, mentoring, training, feedback and evaluation, planning, delegating, managing, problem solving, and resourcing.

SUCCESS IN LEADERSHIP COMES FROM FOCUSING ON THE UNSEEN 90%

ICEBERG IN DETAIL

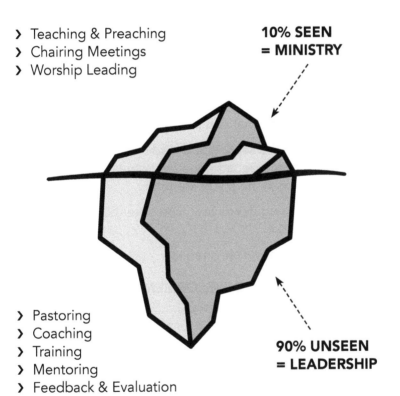

> Teaching & Preaching
> Chairing Meetings
> Worship Leading

10% SEEN = MINISTRY

> Pastoring
> Coaching
> Training
> Mentoring
> Feedback & Evaluation
> Planning & Organising
> Delegating
> Managing
> Directing
> Problem Solving

90% UNSEEN = LEADERSHIP

Success in leadership comes from focusing on the unseen 90%.

The question is not, "how do I develop and grow as a leader?" but rather, "how do I empower others to develop and grow as leaders?"

Develop your Leadership Development Plan

Here are some practical steps to take in starting your Leadership Development Plan:

- List the departments, ministries and areas you are responsible for

- Try and list at least three people in each department, ministry or area that you can 'take with you'

- Break down the serving and leading roles and activities of the departments, ministries and areas into specific tasks to help you identify

- List the training needs for those potential leaders to carry out tasks

- List training resources needed

LEADERSHIP DEVELOPMENT PLAN

Department / Area	Potential Leaders (3)	Training Needs	Training Resources
	• • •		
	• • •		
	• • •		

CHAPTER NINE:

DEVELOPING A VOLUNTEERING CULTURE

Serving God is not a demanding, onerous task, but rather, a privilege and honour to serve God.

God has always required His people to serve Him in building His House through the free-will offering of their time, talents and finances.

> *"Go up to the mountains and bring wood*
> *and build the House,*
> *that I may take pleasure in it and be glorified,*
> *says the Lord."*
> *Haggai 1:8*

One of the signs of the 'Day of God's Power', or revival, is the willing and generous volunteering of God's people. A volunteering and serving spirit is a sign of church health and God's presence among His people.

> *"Your people offer themselves willingly*
> *in the day of your power, in holy array."*
> *Psalm 110:3 (WEB)*

Volunteering has far-reaching implications beyond just doing something. Volunteering reaches right into our hearts and motives.

The patriarch Jacob is a classic example. He had no interest in God, the House of God or spiritual things, until he met God in a dramatic, dream encounter. As a result of this life-transforming experience, he immediately and freely offers God his time, talents and treasures to build the House of God.

> *"Then this stone that I have set up as a sacred stone*
> *will be the house of God,*
> *and I will surely give you back a tenth of*
> *everything you give me."*
> *Genesis 28:22*

From this moment, Jacob's heart is transformed from a taker to a giver. He is set on a path of blessing and destiny because he has put God's House at the centre of his affections.

Just like Jacob, we also are all called to serve Christ freely and it is important to understand that God will never take our service lightly; He will reward our volunteering.

This is because God is generous, kind and benevolent in nature and all through the Scriptures we find that He really looks after His servants.

> *"Let them shout for joy and be glad,*
> *who favor my righteous cause.*
> *Yes, let them say continually, "the Lord be magnified,*
> *who has pleasure in the prosperity of his servant!"*
> *Psalm 35:27*

When we favour God's righteous cause, serving in building God's House, God will favour, bless and prosper us.

WHEN WE BUILD GOD'S HOUSE
GOD WILL BUILD OUR HOUSE

> *"Consider your ways.*
> *Go up to the mountain, bring wood, and*
> *build the house.*
> *I will take pleasure in it, and I will be glorified,"*
> *says Yahweh.*
> *"You looked for much, and, behold, it came to little;*
> *and when you brought it home, I blew it away.*
> *Why?" says Yahweh of Armies,*
> *"Because of my house that lies waste,*
> *while each of you is busy with his own house.*
> *Therefore, for your sake the heavens*
> *withhold the dew,*

and the earth withholds its fruit.
I called for a drought on the land, on the mountains,
on the grain, on the new wine, on the oil,
on that which the ground brings forth,
on men, on livestock, and on all the labour
of the hands."
Haggai 1:7-11

THINGS GO BETTER
WHEN WE MAKE IT A PRIORITY
TO SERVE GOD AND BUILD HIS HOUSE

The revelation of volunteering centres on the understanding that we are not just helping God out, but rather, we are entrusted with a stewardship from God. Therefore, we must all find out where Christ has entrusted us to serve. This is not an optional extra, but a vital part of our spiritual health, growth and progress.

Jesus has not just invited us to work for Him,
but to work with Him. This is the place of rest and
spiritual health.
"Are you tired? Worn out? Burned out on religion?
Come to me. Get away with me and
you'll recover your life.
I'll show you how to take a real rest.
Walk with me and work with me – watch how I do it.
Learn the unforced rhythms of grace.
I won't lay anything heavy or ill-fitting on you.
Keep company with me and you'll learn to
live freely and lightly."
Matthew 11:29-30 (MESSAGE)

The apostle Paul understood that we all have gifts, given by the Holy Spirit, so that we can all serve God effectively:

"Having then gifts
differing according to the grace that is given to us,
whether prophecy, let us prophesy according to the
proportion of faith;
Or ministry, let us wait on our ministering:
or he that teaches, on teaching;
Or he that exhorts, on exhortation:
he that gives, let him do it with simplicity;
he that leads, with diligence;
he that shows mercy, with cheerfulness."
Romans 12:6-8

Discipleship, growth and progress never occur alone or in a vacuum, but always happen best in a context; and that context is serving and volunteering on team in the local church.

"...from which all the body by joints and bands having
nourishment ministered,
and knit together, increases with the
increase of God."
Colossians 2:19

However, when we serve with reluctance or from feeling pressured, problems can arise in our lives like Jonah, for example, who was the reluctant prophet.

He ran away from the will of God and his service, and ended up angry, revengeful and depressed.

"But it displeased Jonah exceedingly, and he
was very angry.
And he prayed unto the LORD, and said,

I pray, O LORD, was not this my saying,
when I was yet in my country?
Therefore I fled before unto Tarshish:
for I knew that you are a gracious God, and merciful,
slow to anger, and of great kindness, and you
repent of the evil.
Therefore now, O LORD, I beseech you,
take my life from me;
for it is better for me to die than to live."
Jonah 4:1,3

Jesus is our great example who came as a servant:

"But you shall not be so:
but he that is greatest among you, let him
be as the younger;
and he that is chief, as he that serves.
For who is greater, he that sits at food,
or he that serves?
is not he that sits at food?
but I am among you as he that serves."
Luke 22:26-27

Church life and leadership is all about volunteering. Without volunteers the church simply could not function and accomplish the great vision of God.

Volunteers are the life-blood of the church and this is why one of the core roles of leadership is to raise up as many volunteers as possible because the harvest is huge and therefore the task is mammoth.

"But when he saw the multitudes, he was moved with
compassion on them,
because they fainted, and were scattered abroad,

*as sheep having no shepherd. Then he said
to his disciples,
The harvest truly is plenteous, but the
laborers are few;
Pray therefore to the Lord of the harvest,
that he will send laborers into his harvest. "
Matthew 9:36-38*

Maximising Your Volunteer Resource

One of the critical skills of a leader is knowing how to attract and win volunteers into service. This is the power of attraction versus the power of repelling at work.

We attract people to our cause and us when we display the following:

- A **pleasant manner** is contagious because there is nothing like a smile to open doors and create a positive atmosphere. When a smile is followed up with pleasant and positive speech, everyone's heart is filled with warmth and happiness.

- **Enthusiasm** is the x-factor that is energetic, positive and urgent. Enthusiasm moves people and is highly contagious.

- **Healthy relationships** that are based on a spirit of serving and reciprocal love are the foundation of attraction. People are drawn in because of the health of the connection.

- **Established systems and procedures** are vital to an organisation or endeavour, especially when they are impartial, create clarity and bring a sense of strategy to everyone involved.

Once we have volunteers, it is essential to mobilise them into action by resourcing them so they know:

- What to do
- How to do it
- Have the means and resources to do it

We can achieve this by providing our volunteers with the following:

- Clear job descriptions and role definitions
- On the job training and coaching

Show your volunteers how to do the job by breaking every role down.

It is important to keep your expectations at a reasonable level so volunteers can actually participate in serving. Also, because people are volunteering, there is always a need for flexibility and fitting the role to the ability, capacity and time availability of the volunteers. By doing this, more people can be involved in serving.

Feedback and Debriefing

Every team member needs opportunity for regular debriefing and feedback after the delivery of ministry and service for continuous improvement and progress.

The Power of Endorsement

Words and actions of endorsement are so important for volunteers because they are not paid, therefore, leaders must find ways to endorse their efforts and commitment.

Some ways to achieve this is through:

- Verbal and written affirmations and appreciation
- Praising and promoting them to others
- Including them in the action
- Finding practical ways to reward them such as gifts, costs for conferences, books and holidays

Supporting our Volunteers

It is important to be present and to help our volunteers. The role of leaders is to make them look great. Leaders can best achieve this by:

- Resourcing them
- Problem solving for them
- Backing them up
- Handling criticism of them
- Encouraging them, because encouraging words are fuel for the soul

Releasing our Volunteers

We have found that it is essential to treat every volunteer as a seasonal worker; in other words, they are with you for a limited time.

Never treat volunteers as your personal property, or "my volunteers", because they're not. They are offering their time, energy and talents freely. It is far better to refer to all volunteers in the church as "our volunteers" and so create an atmosphere that is releasing of people into a new role, a better role, or into another department.

It is important to brag about how good they are and put them forward for consideration when other departments in the church or organisation are in need. That way you will develop a free and empowering style of working with, developing and mobilising volunteers in the kingdom.

CHAPTER TEN:

THE APPROACH AND LANGUAGE OF RAISING LEADERS

One of the core skills needed in raising leaders is the understanding and ability to be able to adopt the right leadership approach, mode and language.

This approach views the development and progress of candidates through the 4 stages of leadership styles, or approaches, such as, pastoring, coaching, mentoring and parenting. These clearly differentiated stages or phases involve the four kinds of approaches such as, establishing, serving, leading and endorsing.

PASTORING = DIRECTIVE

Pastoring is initiated, directed, implemented and maintained by the leader and revolves around connection, nurturing, instruction and involving the new believer into the life of the church.

The core focus of pastoring is the **establishing** of the believer in their faith in Christ and their participation in the church.

The limitation with pastoring is in terms of the development of the believer beyond the foundational stage of Christianity. In other words, if we keep pastoring people, we will only produce and maintain infants in Christ because we are doing everything and providing everything for them.

COACHING = PRESCRIPTIVE

Coaching revolves around the identification of gifts, skills and passions, with the purpose of mobilising the believer into effective service in church life. Coaching requires the submission and cooperation of the believer with their leader. This is a major step forward for the believer to embrace the higher demands of discipleship.

There is no doubt that the involvement in serving creates growth, maturity and progress in the life of the new believer like nothing else. Leadership is never developed in a vacuum...always in a context.

The core focus of coaching is the **training and equipping** of the believer into service (function) and adding value by contributing to the church and others.

The limitation of coaching, in terms of the development of a leader, is located in its focus on the effectiveness of the performance of the servant rather than the development of the character and motivations of the leader. This is where a higher level of approach is required to foster the growth of character alongside the growth of giftings and ability, which I describe as 'charisma', in the candidate.

MENTORING = DESCRIPTIVE

'Mentoring' focuses on the **life development** of the servant/ minister, with a view to **develop leadership potential** in them.

Mentoring requires a higher level of commitment, understanding and initiative on the part of the potential leader. Therefore, the mentor must change his/her approach and language in order to draw the leader out of the mentored person.

Questioning, enquiring, probing and suggesting form the basis of discussion – as opposed to the more directive approach of the pastor and coach.

Mentoring is at its optimum when the potential leader is initiating, enquiring, engaging and implementing with the mentor.

The mentor will engage in all approaches of pastoring, coaching and mentoring in order to facilitate the outcomes of maturity and success of the person they are mentoring.

The core focus of mentoring is the development of the Godly character and internal drivers of the leader. This is the 'kingdom mindset'. Ultimately, leaders are more fruitful and successful in the long-term because of their character rather than their charisma.

Charisma will open doors and take me places, but character will keep me there!

This is the true focus of mentoring, and should be the goal of the leadership process: to be engaged in the development of character and 'kingdom drivers', not just the implementation of Christian ministry.

PARENTING = PREDICTIVE

Most would agree that parenting is one of the highest levels of the human experience because, by its very nature, parenting centres around the selfless commitment of raising and empowering children to stand in their own right and become even more successful in life than their parents.

"Behold, the third time I am ready to come to you; and I will not be burdensome to you: for I seek not yours, but you: for the children ought not to lay up for the parents, but the parents for the children."
2 Corinthians 12:14

A normal, healthy parent would never be threatened by their child's success or want their children to be less, or achieve less than themselves. Rather, the healthy, mature parent is on the sidelines cheering their child on to every success in life!

This is the same with spiritual leadership. The highest level of leadership is to progress beyond just being a pastor, coach or mentor and to become a 'spiritual parent' to others.

> *"For though ye have ten thousand teachers in Christ,*
> *yet you do not have many fathers:*
> *for in Christ Jesus I have begotten you through*
> *the gospel."*
> *1 Corinthians 4:15*

Spiritual parenting revolves around the selfless commitment of raising, empowering and releasing capable leaders to the next level of authority and function in the church and kingdom, and hopefully, to facilitate their progress beyond the level, expertise and success of the mentor.

This is the mark of true success for every leader: that our 'spiritual sons and daughters' progress beyond ourselves and even become our leaders, rather than remaining indefinitely under our authority and sponsorship.

Spiritual parenting requires a high degree of humility and security in order to invest tirelessly into the development of those you've been entrusted with. It requires an even higher degree of humility and security to then release the ones you've been entrusted with to progress to greater levels of leadership and fruitfulness than yourself...and be 100% supportive of it.

The core focus of spiritual parenting is the unreserved endorsement and celebration of their spiritual son or daughter and then to focus again on reproducing another competent and fruitful leader.

> *"I have no greater joy than this,*
> *to hear about my children walking in truth."*
> *3 John 1:4*

CHAPTER ELEVEN:

FOUR SKILLS OF GROWING LEADERS

The first skill to develop in growing leaders is the ability to identify potential in others. This is what sets leaders apart: their ability to see what others don't see. It is that combination of what is 'prophetic' (spiritual insight) and what is 'potential' (seeing traits, passions and abilities).

Leaders possess an intuitive ability to see the potential in others. They see potential in situations, environments and in people.

Leaders see hearts, because they see themselves first. In other words, they understand people's motivations, strengths and weaknesses.

Because of this insight, leaders tend to build on strengths, which is the opposite to the 'mercy' spiritual gift, which wants to help others in their weakness.

Leaders see what needs to be done and are able to convert lack, problems and needs into practical plans of action. While seeing what needs to be done tends to be complicated to others, this is a simple matter to a leader.

A simple key to effective leadership is learning to keep your eyes open. The way we can do this is to look for the potential in others by using the 'FAST' method:

Faithful — love God and people constantly

Available — in all seasons of life

Servant-hearted — demonstrates a serving spirit to leaders and people

Teachable — open-hearted, allows access into personal word

The second skill to develop in growing leaders is the ability to develop others.

You can begin this journey by making a list of the people you are developing and find practical ways in which to include people in what you are already doing.

By opening these opportunities to those you are seeking to develop, you are contextualising what you are teaching by 'doing life together'. The developing of others takes time, resources, energy and emotion.

Learning how to methodically delegate responsibilities is vital to developing others. It is not about dumping what you don't want to do onto others, or what is too difficult for you to do, rather, inspiring others to commit to the same personal level of demand you live by while encouraging them to live a higher, stronger and more fruitful life.

The third skill to develop in growing leaders is the ability to release others by creating opportunities.

So where do opportunities exist? Opportunities exist in the multitude of needs that exist around us everywhere, everyday, and leadership is all about meeting those needs.

Here are some ideas on creating a need-meeting approach:

- Identify needs based on vision – "what are we called to do here?"
- Know what needs to be done – come up with a plan and a list of needs.
- Match people to fulfill needs – identify and recruit the right people that can meet the needs.

- Hold those leaders accountable to agreed outcomes based on meeting needs, rather than on subjective feelings by de-personalising leadership and roles.

The fourth skill to develop in growing leaders is the ability to follow up.

However, before effective follow up can happen, the leader needs to create:

- A culture of serving and involvement – "we're making God's House great."

- A culture of encouragement – "I believe in you."

- A culture of accountability – "I will follow you up and give feedback."

Once this kind of culture is created, the leader can more effectively follow up by:

- Monitoring performance and delivery

- Giving appropriate feedback and evaluation

- Agreeing on adjustments and progress

- Resetting agreed outcomes

The best leadership learning and development opportunities occur in the 'follow up moments'. We developed at our church a practice of holding regular follow up meetings to give feedback, especially after the delivery of ministry and service by all leaders.

The Power of Feedback

We all need help from an objective person who believes in us, to identify our areas for improvement as we seek to progress in life. All great athletes, business people and leaders have coaches. This is why we have prioritised and incorporated feedback opportunities for all our leaders as part of their leadership development process.

As human beings we don't always see things clearly, or even know how to implement adjustments that will bring the best out in us. This is why we need a coach, a mentor and an overseer to help us by providing constructive feedback.

The trouble with blindspots is we don't see them

The goal of positive feedback from a trusted coach/ mentor/overseer is to develop our ability to self analyse and self adjust. This is called maturity. Once we learn the skills of self-analysis and self-adjustment, we are able to be self-maintaining. This is the creation of a healthy and productive leader.

The most important contributor to maximising the help of an overseer, coach and mentor is to be teachable. This is the ability to receive input, and learn new things that will propel us into a positive and more productive future.

Great Mentors and Coaches Ask Questions

Successful mentors and coaches know how to ask the right questions in order to draw out answers and solutions from within the person being mentored. The competent and skillful mentor already knows the answer, but understands the importance of the journey of discovery through asking the right questions.

The best kind of questions never require a simple "yes" or "no" answer, but rather provoke thinking. These kinds of questions unearth a more detailed and accurate response because they require responses that involve processing, analysis, application and conclusions.

In the case of giving feedback to a new preacher, for example, the coach would ask questions like; "What two things did you do well?" "What two things do you think you didn't do so well?" "Do you think you achieved our agreed outcomes?" "What could you improve on for the next time you speak?" "What do you think about these observations and ideas I have that could help you?"

CHAPTER TWELVE:

RAISING NEXT GENERATION LEADERS

*"I thank God, whom I serve with a pure conscience,
as my forefathers did,
as without ceasing I remember you in my prayers
night and day,
greatly desiring to see you, being mindful of your
tears, that I may be filled with joy,
when I call to remembrance the genuine faith
that is in you,
which dwelt first in your grandmother Lois and your
mother Eunice,
and I am persuaded is in you also.
Therefore, I remind you to stir up the gift of God
which is in you
through the laying on of my hands.
For God has not given us a spirit of fear,
but of power and of love and of a sound mind."
2 Timothy 1:3-7 NKJV*

Raising next generation leaders is the most important activity that any leader can focus on and give attention to because it secures the future health and viability of the church.

We do this when we move from viewing the next generation as just the kids and youth in their programs, to including next generation leaders in the main church.

What we focus on grows. Therefore, if we focus on raising next generation leaders, that's exactly what we'll get: next generation leaders flourishing in the House of God.

It is essential that as leaders we genuinely include the next generation in our hearts, not just in our 'program' because we genuinely have a care and love of young people.

We do this when we follow the example of the apostle Paul

who "included them in his prayers" (2 Timothy 1:3-5) and included them in his life.

Giving attention to the next generation is essential, and the best way we can do this is by encouraging them, endorsing them and affirming their spiritual heritage, journey and experience as valid and important.

- Their 'heritage' = where they got it from

- Their 'experience' = what they've got

- Their 'journey' = how far they've come

> *"When I call to remembrance the genuine faith*
> *that is in you,*
> *which dwelt first in your grandmother Lois, and your*
> *mother Eunice;*
> *and I am persuaded that in you also."*
> *1 Timothy 1:5*

Including the next generation in the church's mentoring and coaching activities in their teenage years really sets them up spiritually and paves the way for taking on significant roles and positions in the church after they have graduated from school.

The core focus of our mentoring program has always been on the development of Godly character and spiritual disciplines.

The key to unlocking leadership in a young person is to help them discover their spirituality

We also observe this focus by the apostle Paul, writing to the young leader Timothy, where he lists fifteen qualifications of leaders (1 Timothy 3), of which fourteen are 'spiritual and practical', and one, 'giftedness' ("able to teach").

Why is this emphasis important?

Because it is clear that a person's charisma, or giftedness, can't take them beyond their character, or their ability to sustain and maintain their gifts.

Here's the deal. People who last and finish well in leadership have developed sufficient character to sustain and maintain the opportunities that their giftedness provided for them.

This is why it is vital to make the growth and development of character more important than the exercise and display of gifts in the mentoring of young leaders.

The core reasons for this emphasis is firstly found in the fact that character, or righteous living, takes more time to develop than charisma, because charisma is the 'instant' endowment of a gift, while character is developed through a process, and secondly, the fruits of character are far more rewarding and honoring to God in the long run.

> *"But the wisdom that is from above is first pure,*
> *then peaceable, gentle, and easy to be entreated,*
> *full of mercy and good fruits, without partiality, and*
> *without hypocrisy.*
> *And the fruit of righteousness is sown in peace of*
> *them that make peace."*
> *James 3:17-18*

Leaders are not 'ready made'; they are developed over time. Leaders don't come from 'there', imported from elsewhere; they are 'here', already within the church.

When we try to circumvent the process of developing leaders from among the people God has given us, we will create a 'hireling spirit' among leaders, where people will seek to be employed for payment rather than serving freely and willingly for the love of God's house.

One of the best ways to raise next generation leaders is to encourage them.

All through his letters to Timothy, Paul encourages him to be confident and strong in his faith, leadership and ministry. Success in raising leaders is multiplied in an environment of encouragement.

We encourage others by our attitude, our words and our actions. When we are big-hearted, affirming, confirming, supporting, resourcing and opening doors of opportunity for young leaders, they will flourish around us.

> *"That our sons may be as plants grown up*
> *in their youth;*
> *that our daughters may be as corner stones,*
> *polished after the similitude of a palace."*
> *Psalm 144:12*

The PAR-EXCELLENT
Leader...

THE LEADER WHO EMPOWERS OTHERS TO BE THE BEST THEY CAN BE!

"Whoever wants to be great among you
must be your servant,
and whoever wants to be first among you
must be your slave –
Even as the Son of man
came not to be served, but to serve,
and to give his life a ransom for many."

Matthew 20:28